THE PETIT TRIANON AND THE QUEEN'S HAMLET VISITOR'S GUIDE

Christian Baulez

Head Curator

artlys

Editorial co-ordination : Denis Kilian
Layout : Martine Mène
Editorial follow-up and picture research : Christian Ryo
Production : Pierre Kegels

4 rue Saint-Fiacre
78000 Versailles

ISBN 2-85495-079-8

CONTENTS

General plan of the Versailles estate 4
Plan of the Petit Trianon and the Queen's Hamlet . . 6
Introduction 8

The château du Petit Trianon

The courtyard of the Petit Trianon and the chapel . . 12
The grand staircase and the antechamber 14
The grand dining room 16
The small dining room 20
The guest Drawing room 22
The Queen's chamber 26
The mechanical mirror room 28
The dressing room with chairs and the bathroom . . . 30
The King's apartment 32

The french Garden 36
The Queen's theatre 38
The ring game and the english Garden 40
The Temple of Love 42

The Queen's Hamlet

The Mill 44
The Queen's Cottage 46
The Pigeon loft, the guard house
and the Marlborough Tower 48
The Farm 50
The Belvedere 52
The Charpentier garden and the Richard house . . . 54

The Petit Trianon

The Queen's Hamlet

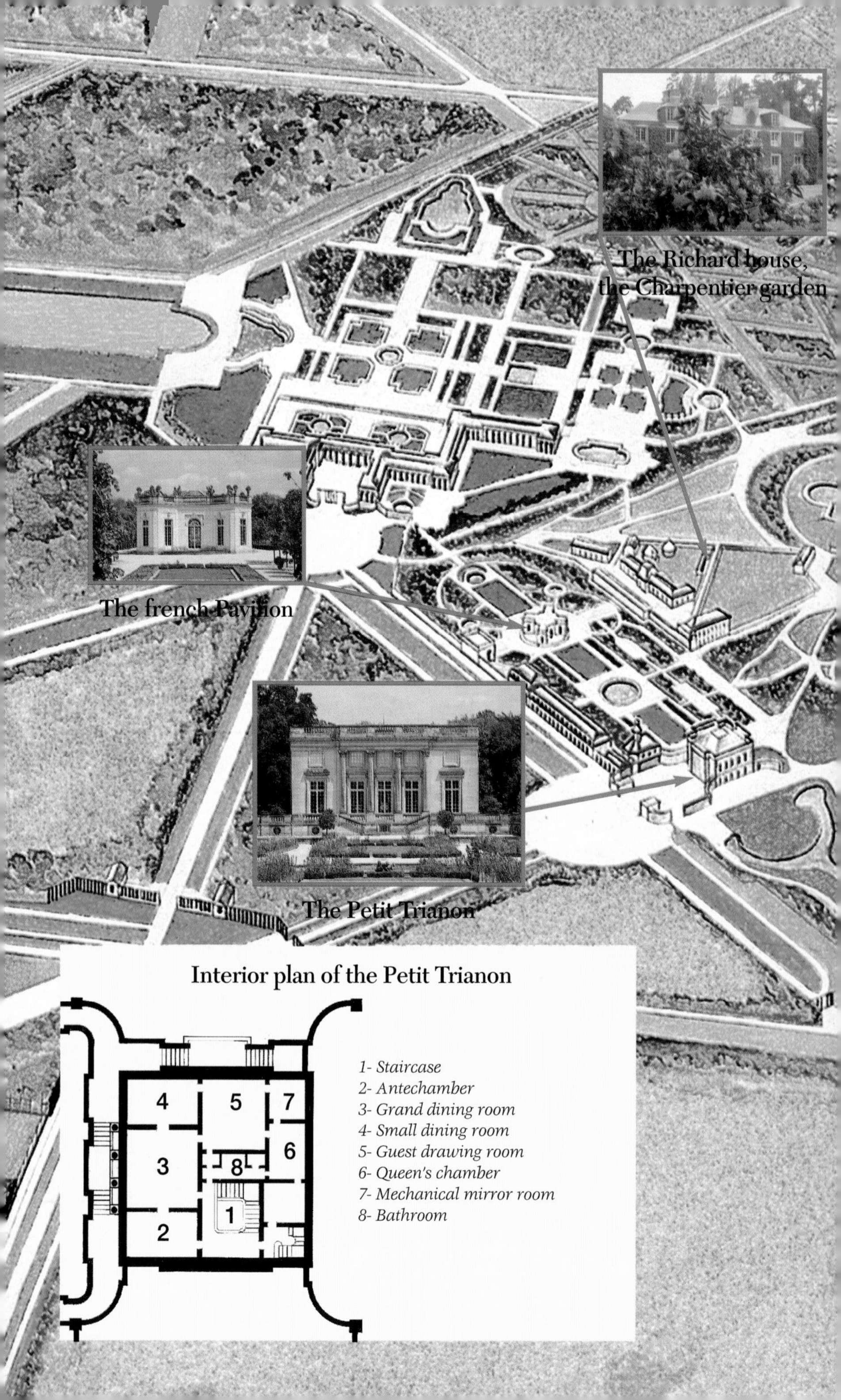
The Richard house,
the Charpentier garden
The french Pavilion
The Petit Trianon
Interior plan of the Petit Trianon
1- Staircase
2- Antechamber
3- Grand dining room
4- Small dining room
5- Guest drawing room
6- Queen's chamber
7- Mechanical mirror room
8- Bathroom

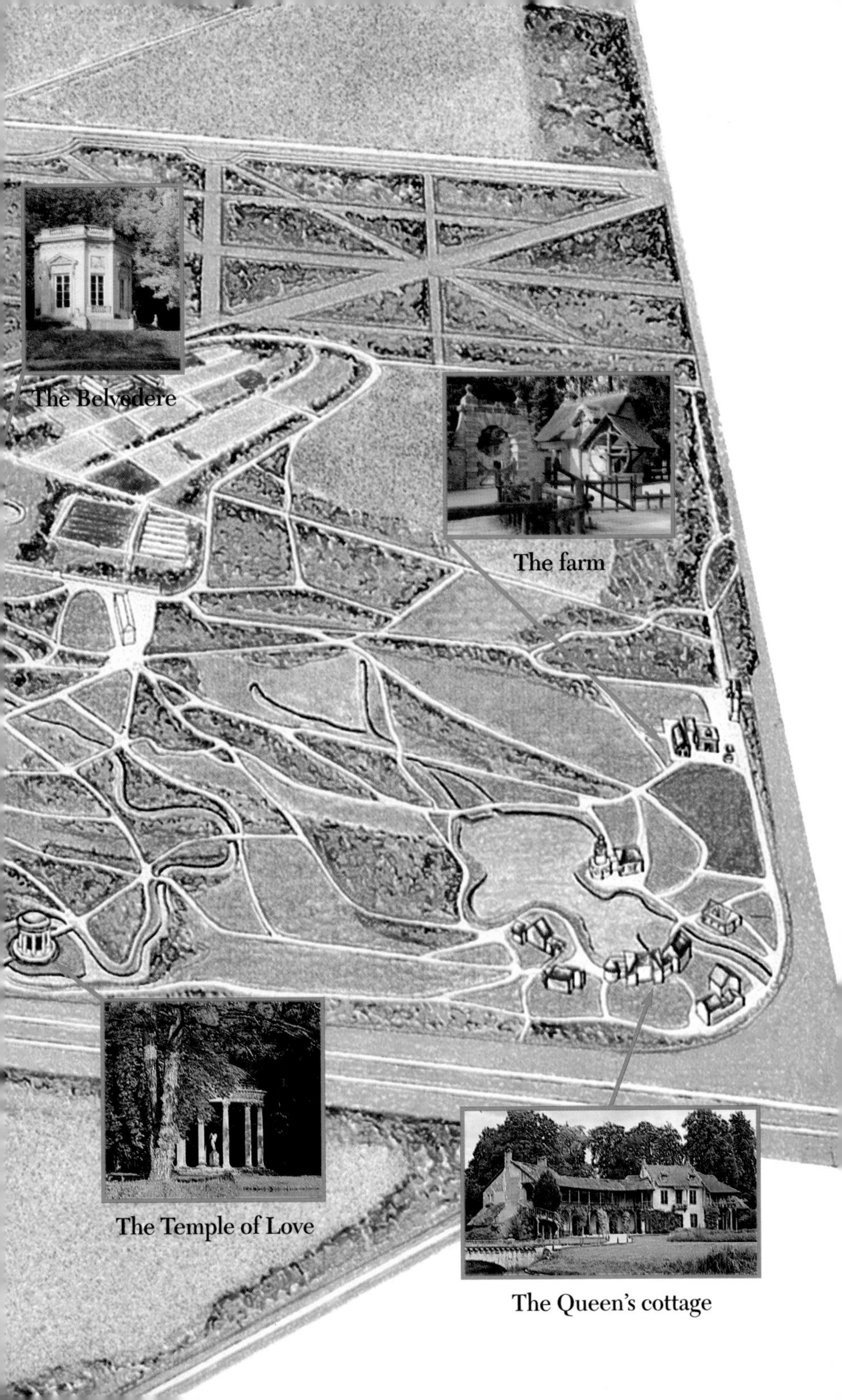
The Belvedere
The farm
The Temple of Love
The Queen's cottage

It was in a relatively out-of-the-way part of the Trianon Palace estate, which had either been left as a meadow or turned into a nursery, that Louis XV had a small private garden planted in 1749. The King rediscovered the charm of the Trianon which he had grown to love as a child and where, as an adult, he amused and educated himself under the influence of the Marquise de Pompadour. Thus, he gradually created a veritable botanical garden whose fame soon spread, and which prompted him to have a small chateau built to take greater advantage of it.

While at the nearby palace, he had two fashionable apartments converted for the use of the Marquise and himself, and in 1749, Louis XV ordered a new menagerie accommodating domestic animals to be built and a new garden planted.

The garden comprised fig trees, a vegetable garden, a flower garden and shortly thereafter, hothouses for flowers and exotic and delicate fruits. Gardeners Claude and Antoine Richard, father and son, managed the garden in turn, and in 1759, Bernard Jussieu, was able to pursue his work on the classification of plants. The garden soon boasted over 4,000 different plants, often brought back from expeditions to distant lands.

At the same time, Ange-Jacques Gabriel, the chief architect to the King, added two charming pavilions: in 1750, the French Pavilion situated at the intersection of the new garden whose main purpose was games and light refreshment, and the following year, the dining room known as the Cool Summer Drawing Room, and sheltered by a small group of trees.

Madame Du Barry taking her coffee, after J.B. Gautier-Dagoty, circa 1771

This charming new garden led Louis XV to start planning a small chateau in 1758 where he could stay with a only privileged few and would be able to spend the night without mobilising a great number of servants. The Seven Years' War (1756-1763) delayed proceedings, and preliminary planning did not start in earnest until 1761, with work commencing the following year. The building was covered in 1764 and, in 1768, the interior decoration was completed. Work did not start on the chapel until 1772.

The Marquise de Pompadour who was behind the project, and her brother, the Marquis de Marigny, general director of the King's buildings, had insisted that the little chateau be in the latest fashion, known at that time as "à la grecque" or "in the Grecian style". The Petit Trianon was to be the masterpiece of the renaissance of neo-classicism, and no money or talent was spared in its execution. A.-J. Gabriel was surrounded by a new entourage, notably the sculptor Honoré Guibert, to translate into an official style the audacious designs of the fashionable ornemanistes such as Jean-François de Neufforge and Jean Charles Delafosse. The death of Madame de Pompadour in 1764 prevented her from seeing the completion of the little chateau, which was inaugurated five years later by Louis XV and the Countess Du Barry, his new favourite. The sumptuous interior decoration and furnishings were co-ordinated and in the very latest style. Although there was little gilding in this chateau which was dedicated to nature, an abundance of flowers was scattered throughout, on the panelling by Guibert, the chairs by the Foliots, the bronzes from Quentin Claude Pitoin and the cabinetwork from Gilles Joubert.

It was at the Chateau de Trianon that, in the spring of 1774, Louis XV felt the first symptoms of the illness which would bring him to Versailles on the 10th of May. On the following 15th of August, Marie-Antoinette, now Queen of France, received from her husband a passe-partout decorated with 531 diamonds making her the mistress of the estate. From that moment on and for the next fifteen years, she used the Trianon as her private retreat where she could relax away from the luxury of the Court, indulge in her favourite pastimes and hold parties for her relatives and close friends, just as Louis XV did. In the Chateau de Trianon, she gave her own orders; everything was done "by order of the Queen", and it soon came to be known as "Little Vienna" which gave rise to considerable feelings of ill will.

Having little time for botany, Marie-Antoinette ordered the collections compiled by Louis XV to be transferred immediately to the Jardin des Plantes in Paris, and had designed in its place, a garden in the then fashionable Anglo-Chinese style. The Duc de Croÿ, who had known the Trianon well at the time of the late King, expressed his surprise in 1780. "In the place of the great hothouse (the most scholarly and the most expensive in Europe), there are now quite high hills, a large rock and a river. Never before have two acres of land been so transformed, nor cost so much money." Jussieu was now succeeded by the painter Hubert Robert,

The last portrait of Louis XV, painted in March 1774, by Arnauld-Vincent de Montpetit

who was more suited to creating picturesque viewpoints, although this did not prevent the Richards from continuing their research into rare species.

Richard Mique, the architect from Lorraine, who had worked in Nancy for King Stanislas and then for Queen Marie Leczinska, was henceforth responsible for the new constructions: a Chinese ring game built in 1776, the Temple of Love, the Rock Pavilion and the theatre, built between 1777 and 1779. There was soon a lack of available space, and in 1783, Mique had to go beyond the boundaries of the garden to build a fantasy hamlet intended for rustic and domestic activities.

The Temple of Love in the English Garden, water-colour by L. -N. de Lespinasse, circa 1780

This hamlet did not have a chapel of its own, although beyond it, one could make out the nearby bell tower of Saint-Antoine du Buisson, built on the edge of the avenue marking the bounding of the gardens of the Trianon on the western side. In 1786, Richard Mique erected the Saint-Antoine gate to add to the splendour of this entrance to the royal domain. Calling to mind a triumphal arch, it can still be seen today.

After a good many hesitations, the Revolution spared the Queen's retreat, although all the contents were sold as of 1793, including the mirrors, their gilded frames and the fireplaces from the hamlet. The upkeep of the chateau slowed down, or rather it was badly maintained by the tenants, who were eager, above all, to attract strollers to this still enchanting place now converted into an inn where public dances were held.

THE FIRST EMPIRE 1804-1815

From 1805, Napoleon I restored order here and elsewhere, evicting the tenants and ordering repair work to make the premises habitable. Restored, repainted, endowed with new mirrors and refurnished, the Petit Trianon was allotted to the Emperor's sister, Pauline, wife of Prince Borghèse. In 1810, the new empress, Archduchess Marie-Louise, niece of Marie-Antoinette, discovered her aunt's retreat, which she enjoyed more and more with each stay at the neighbouring palace of Grand Trianon. For her benefit, efforts were made to re-establish the fantasies of the past by installing a new Chinese ring game and restoring the theatre. In 1811, the hamlet was also restored as much as possible.

THE RESTORATION 1815-1830

Louis XVIII, restored to the throne of his forefathers, showed little interest in the former retreat of his sister-in-law Marie-Antoinette, but was mainly preoccupied with removing any Napoleonic traces. His legacy includes, above all, a commission to the painter François-Louis Dejuinne in 1819 for four large allegorical paintings depicting the seasons, destined to replace those in the dining room which had been lost during the Revolution. In June 1816, when the King held a dazzling dinner in honour of Marie-Caroline of Naples, great-niece of the late Queen, who married the Duc de Berry, future heir to the throne, all thoughts were doubtless on Marie-Antoinette once again.

The July Monarchy 1830-1848

The furniture was still that of Pauline Borghèse and the Empress Marie-Louise when Louis-Philippe decided, in 1836, to pass on the Petit Trianon to his eldest son, the Duke of Orleans, who was about to marry Princess Hélène of Mecklenburg. The entire chateau was renewed and equipped with modern comforts. The furnishings were completed to meet the needs of a couple and a large staff. The Duke and Duchess of Orleans were the last royalty to stay in the chateau.

The Second Empire 1851-1870

It was not until the Exposition universelle of 1867 that the Petit Trianon found another function. The Empress Eugénie, who worshipped the memory of Marie-Antoinette, decided to remove all traces of her predecessors and turn the chateau into a museum dedicated to the memory of the Queen. She had pieces of furniture and objets d'art which had (allegedly) belonged to Marie-Antoinette, removed from the royal residences and even taken from the Imperial furniture store. All of these were gathered together at the Petit Trianon which thus became, like Malmaison which was dedicated to the Empress Joséphine, one of the first attempts at historical refurnishing.

The Republic today

Since then, generations of historians, architects, gardeners and curators have been trying, through their research, their work and their acquisitions, to improve the presentation of the chateau and render it even more in keeping with its original state, as revealed by studies of archive material. The first-floor walls of

Illumination of the rock and the Belvedere in August 1781 for the visit of Joseph II by Cl.-L. Châtelet

the chateau recently regained their original colour, a very pale water-green on a white background, framed with sculpted flowers for the mirrors and above the doors, the design having been drawn on the walls behind the panelling. The hamlet and the gardens, last restored in the inter-war years thanks to considerable donations from John D. Rockefeller and his heirs, is currently the subject of new restoration work. The installation of heating in the houses should also allow furniture originally commissioned for Empress Marie-Louise to be exhibited.

Regardless of which side you approach it, the Petit Trianon appears as a square pavilion with twenty-three metre sides, five windows per façade per storey, with a bel étage on the ground floor and an attic. The subtle use of steps compensates for differences in level. Only the façade facing the former botanical garden is not decorated with classical orders. Elsewhere the Corinthian order is used, either on pilasters on two of the façades or on detached columns on the main façade facing the French Garden. The chateau is crowned with a baluster concealing the flat roof.

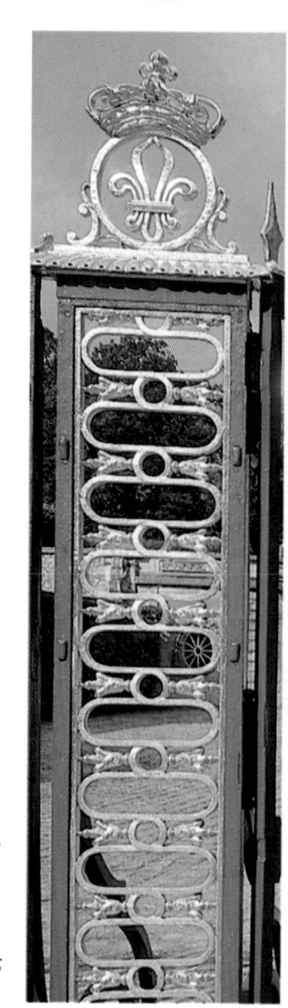

A beautiful grille between two sentry boxes gives access to the entrance courtyard. Two walls, concealed by shrubs, separate this courtyard from the garden to the right and the outbuildings to the left.

To the left of the courtyard, the chapel erected by Gabriel in 1772-73 and crowned with a picturesque onion-shaped bell-tower stands out against the sky. In the 19th century, a clock by Lepaute replaced the clock made by Robert Robin in 1785 on the orders of Marie-Antoinette which is now housed in the Musée d'Histoire Naturelle.

The interior of the chapel, which is not normally open to visitors, is covered in sober grey panelling. The high altar with its two Ionic columns supports a pediment with a Gothic "Christ in Glory" sculpted by Joseph Prévôt; a 1774 painting by Joseph-Marie Vien depicting Saint Louis and Marguerite de Provence visiting Saint Thibault, the subject having been chosen by Louis XV himself in 1767; and a basket of lilies being presented by the saint to the sovereigns symbolising the posterity of the Bourbons. Louis-Philippe had two further groups added in 1847 in the lateral niches - "l'Éducation de la Vierge" (the education of the Virgin) by Julien Gourdel in 1844 and "Jésus au jardin des oliviers" (Jesus in Gethsemane) by Jacques-Augustin Dieudonné in 1846.

Visitors enter the castle through the right-hand door into the former billiard room where the visitor reception is today and proceed to the Grand Stairway with its exquisite tiled floor in white veined and green Campan marble. Green is the prevailing colour of the Trianon, while flowers are its main ornamentation. Visitors are most struck by the superb banisters of the staircase, the work of the ironsmith François Brochois, where the initials M.A. for Marie-Antoinette replaced the two interlaced LL of Louis XV.

Honoré Gilbert created all the sculptures completed in 1765 and, notably, between the windows, the Head of Medusa "which seems to forbid unwanted guests from entering" (Pierre de Nolhac). The windows themselves, like all the windows on this floor, were initially large-paned, a rare luxury in the time of Louis XV.

The Antechamber, illuminated by two windows facing the entrance court and a French window opening onto the French Garden, was originally heated by two monumental earthenware stoves, which Marie-Antoinette had removed to make way for two false glass doors. Louis-Philippe then substituted two sculpted panels from the Cool Summer Drawing Room of the French Garden. The current doors are a contemporary restoration. The cabinets are by J.-H. Riesener, the cabinet maker of the royal furniture store.

The decoration above the doors conforms to a programme finalised in 1768 by Charles-Nicolas Cochin, secretary of the Academy. "It is in this secondary residence that the King keeps his most beautiful flowers; above the doors, I searched for subjects with flowers, taken from Ovid's *"Metamorphoses..."* Thus it is Ovid who served as the main theme for Jean-Philippe Caresme to paint *"Menthe changée en herbe"* and *"Mirrha changée en Mirthe"*. Only the second painting could be found.

Visitors are greeted by a portrait of Marie-Antoinette holding a rose (above) painted by Louise-Elisabeth Vigée Le Brun in 1783. The two marble busts created by Louis-Simon Boizot in 1777 were placed here by order of the Queen - they are of Louis XVI, her husband, (opposite) and Joseph II, her brother, the future emperor.

The Grand Dining Room overlooks the French Garden through three windows. All its decoration revolves around the theme of the fruits of the earth. Above the doors on the antechamber side and opposite side are *"Zéphyr et Flore, Borée et Orythie"* painted by Charles Monnet, on either side of the fireplace are *"Vertumne et Pomone"* and *"Vénus et Adonis"* by Clément Belle. The mahogany chairs were made in 1787 by George Jacob after the designs of the painter Hubert Robert for the drawing room of the Queen's dairy at Rambouillet.

The two consoles between the windows, by Martin Carlin, were confiscated in 1794 from the Marquise de Brunoy, émigrée; they support two Niderwiller bisques brought under Louis-Philippe from the Chateau des Rohan in Strasbourg where they may have been acquired as furniture for Napoleon.

Louis XV, who dined here for the first time on the 11th of September, 1769, intended to have an occasional table in this dining room and the next, designed to bring up all the food to be served from the basement. Reduced scale models were designed by the engineer Antoine-Joseph Loriot, but the state of the royal finances prevented them from being realised in full size. There were also chairs for forty-nine guests.

Honoré Guibert, who designed the panelling, created decoration in keeping with the spirit of the chateau, in other words, dedicated entirely to nature so that the interior of the building would be in harmony with the exterior, remarkable because of the diversity of the sometimes exotic flora, recalling the existence of Louis XV's botanical garden.

On the antechamber side, two large murals on one wall depict *"La Moisson"* (the harvest) by Louis Lagrenée the Elder and *"La Pêche"* (fishing) by Gabriel Doyen, and on the opposite wall, *"La Vendange"* (the grape harvest) by Noël Hallé and *"La Chasse"* (hunting) by Joseph-Marie Vien. Marie-Antoinette, who did not appreciate the nudity in these paintings at all, replaced two of them with paintings sent from Vienna by Empress Maria-Theresa and kept to this day in the Chateau of Versailles: they depict her dancing with her brothers on the occasion of the wedding of Joseph II.

"La Moisson ou Cérès et Triptolème" (the harvest or Ceres and Triptolemus) by L. Lagrenée the Elder (detail)

"La Chasse" (hunting) by Joseph-Marie Vien (detail)

The bust in Sèvres bisque on the mantelpiece depicting Marie-Antoinette in 1775, then aged twenty and in the first year of her reign, created after the work of L.-S. Boizot.

"Early in the morning
I visited the Petit Trianon
of the Queen. My goodness,
such a charming walk!
Those beautiful groves scented
with lilac, inhabited
by nightingales!
The weather was lovely,
the air was balmy, the butterflies
were stretching their golden wings
in the rays of the spring sunshine.
Never in my life have I spent
a more enchanting time
than those three hours
visiting this retreat.
The Queen passes the greater part
of the summer there,
and I consider it a marvel."
Memoirs of the
Baron of Oberkirch,
23 May, 1782.

The turquin blue fireplace sculptures by Jacques-François Dropsy.

The small dining room was furnished like the grand dining room but with only nineteen chairs, one of which was slightly higher than the rest, for the King. The Italian griotte fireplace, omitted from the initial commission in 1766, was provided by J.-F. Dropsy from his own stores - it is the only one on this floor not in the latest fashion. Above the door and the mirror, Antoine Renou had painted Cupids and Graces, which have not been found. They have been replaced by three rural scenes painted by Jean-Baptiste Pater.

The Comtesse du Barry depicted with flowers, porcelain bust, circa 1775. She and Louis XV inaugurated the small chateau built at the instigation of the Marquise de Pompadour.

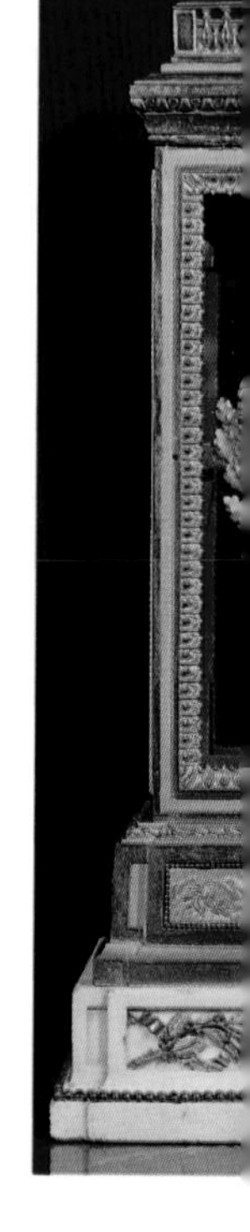

In 1784, Marie-Antoinette had this room turned into her billiard room, but none of the furniture has been found. The pieces seen by visitors today are recent acquisitions and all bear the marks of the Queen's furniture store: chairs by Adrien-Pierre Dupain, chest of drawers and console by J.-H. Riesener. The other furnishings also come from the former royal collections: light bases attributed to Quentin-Claude Pitoin, circa 1775, and ostrich eggs mounted in carved wood, circa 1780.

The Marquise de Pompadour painted "in a summer garden" by Carle Van Loo, circa 1760. With the portrait of the King painted in March 1774 by Armand-Vincent de Montpetit (see page 9), it calls to mind the generation of Louis XV, the generation that created the Petit Trianon.

The cage-clock by Nicolas Sotiau, probably delivered in 1788 for the council chamber of Louis XVI at Saint-Cloud.

The Guest Drawing Room, overlooking the former flower garden, is the main room on this storey.
The recent renovation of this room has resulted in the mirror frames and the paintings being restored and various plans presented to the King being found under the panelling. It transpires that the King had a choice for the lower medallions of the panelling between a monogram in flowers and crowned by the same, a monogram under a royal crown, or a monogram of leaves entwining three ungilded fleurs de lis under a crown of flowers; Louis XV chose the latter, which was both the most royal and the least heraldic, perfectly illustrating the spirit of the Trianon, a royal retreat dedicated to flowers. The monogram of the King in leaves, wich was cut in 1795, has just been restored.

Of the furniture belonging to Louis XV, only a quadrille table in cherry and amaranth threads supplied by Gilles Joubert in 1768 could be repurchased in 1985. The Foliot pieces (a sofa, six armchairs, nineteen chairs, a screen and a partition) have all disappeared, as well as the console table by Guibert and the sumptuous chest of drawers by Joubert, whose violet brèche marbles matched those of the fireplace, the lights by Pitoin and the wall clock by Jean-Antoine Lépine. In their absence, visitors can admire the chairs by J.-B.-Cl. Sené, two wing chairs and a screen by M.-Q. Foliot supplied in 1771 for Madame du Barry at the Chateau de Saint-Hubert. The two chaises voyeuses (low chairs with padded back rail) and the low upholstered chair by G. Jacob were created in 1786 for the Versailles pavilion of the Comte de Provence and his mistress, Madame de Balbi.

The four paintings above the doors also feature the Metamorphoses: "Narcisse changé en fleur" (Narcissus transformed into a flower) and "Adonis changé en anémone" (Adonis transformed into an anemone) by Nicolas Lépicié, to the left and the right of the fireplace respectively; "Clytie changée en tournesol" (Clytia transformed into a sunflower) and "Hyacinthe changé en fleur" (Hyacinth transformed into a flower) by Nicolas-Réné Jollain, on the opposite wall.

The centre of the room is occupied by a pedestal table attributed to Bernard Molitor and supporting an ostrich egg painted by Jean-Étienne Lebel - this egg is from the collections of Madame Adélaïde, daughter of Louis XV, who would have turned the stand. The Savonnerie carpet, partly dating from the 18th century, is of a design by Pierre-Josse Perrot supplied for Marie Leczinska in 1738 and reproduced for the Dauphine Marie-Josèphe of Saxony.

The Guest Drawing Room also has a superb collection of gilt bronzes, with three light holders supplied by Pierre-Philippe Thomire in 1787 for the Games Room of Louis XVI at Saint-Cloud. However, the masterpiece of the genre remains the lantern created for this drawing room on the orders of Marie-Antoinette, probably by the same bronzesmith, in 1785. Sold during the Revolution, it was repurchased by Napoleon I, who had it placed in the pavilion in the French Garden.

Music, like games, features very prominently in this room, both in the carved trophies at the top of the panelling and in the exhibited instruments: a harp, a piano-forte by Pascal Taskin in 1790, and a music stand carved by Gilles-Pierre Cauvet for Princess Kinski (1779) and confiscated at her death in 1794. The celebrated organ clock depicting the Aurora, created by Antoine Wolff circa 1775, was thought for many years to have belonged to Marie-Antoinette, but was actually used by an inspector at the furniture store of the Crown in Paris.

After the Guest Drawing Room, we come to a series of mezzanine rooms illuminated by windows giving onto the former Botanical Garden, which at the time of Marie-Antoinette was turned into the English Garden, with its Temple of Love as the focal point. In 1772, the private chamber of Louis XV became the chamber of the Comtesse Du Barry, who had, until then, occupied an apartment in the attic. In 1776, it became Marie-Antoinette's chamber and, in 1787, was refurnished from the Queen's private furniture store.

The wooden pieces are by G. Jacob, carved with flowers and ears of corn by Pierre-Claude Triquet and Jean-Baptiste-Simon Rode, painted life-size by Jean-Baptiste Chaillot of Prussia. They have kept their original dimity embroidered with wool by Marie-Olivier Desfrages in Lyon. This piece illustrates perfectly the picturesque and supposedly rustic genre cultivated by the Queen at Trianon. The bed, however, has disappeared.

Between the windows, the mahogany and bronze gilded console was created especially by Ferdinand Schwerdfeger in 1788. Also sold on the orders of the Convention in 1793, it was subjected to a second wave of revolution when it was confiscated from Prince Youssoupov in 1917, was confiscated again by the Soviet government in 1933 and was finally bought back by the Versailles museum in 1976. The accompanying writing desk was bequeathed by another Russian, Baron Basile Schlichting, to the Musées Nationaux français.

P.-P. Thomire, bronzesmith to the Queen, also created in 1788, a set of bronze furnishings in the same latticework style. You can see on the fireplace the mechanical eaglet clock by R. Robin which, exceptionally, was not sold in 1793 (assorted light bases can be found at the Gulbenkian Foundation in Lisbon).

Amongst the other furniture, the marquetry country washstand was created in 1784 by J.-H Riesener for Marie-Antoinette's apartment at the Tuileries.
The tulip girandoles in the Parisian porcelain vases were confiscated in 1794 from an emigrée, Adélaïde de Montmorency-Laval.

Through the door to the left, visitors can catch a glimpse of the so-called Mechanical Mirror Room, situated at the corner of the building. Here, Louis XV had his superposed back rooms, linked by a private staircase leading from the ground floor to the attic. One of them served as a coffee r For these most private of room F. Brochois had designed a complex system of locks, so "when the King locked the second door, no key coul it". These rooms linked by the staircase were removed in 1776 and replaced, on this floor, by an interior room. The room could be direct accessed from the steps leading up from the former flower garden. In 1776, the Queen commissioned the mechanic Jean-Tobie Mercklein with the mechanical mirrors which could be raised from the basement to block off the two windows and create a double game of mirrors. This mechanism which was sold in 1793, was restored to run on electric power in 1985. In 1787, Marie-Antoinette commissioned new panelling, richly carved by the Rousseau brothers in the arabesque style, and painted white on a blue background in the style of Wedgwood cameos.

The fireplace clock depicting the theme of "the tearful bird" model in bronze by François Vion, with mechanism by J.-A. Lépine, is identical to that of the Queen at the Trianon. Each side is adorned with two busts in Sèvres bisque depicting Catherine the Great and her son Paul I of Russia, who visited the Trianon in 1782.

A new suite of furniture, probably designed by the ornemaniste Jean-Démosthène Dugourc, was ordered from G. Jacob at this time by the Queen's furniture store. As it has been lost, visitors now see other chairs by G. Jacob himself, which even Marie-Antoinette would not have found disagreeable. They were delivered in 1785 for the pavilion of the Comte de Provence and Madame de Balbi at Versailles. They have been re-upholstered in accordance with their original state, with blue, grey and white so-called "cyclops" lampas, created that same year by the workshop of Reboul and Fontebrune in Lyon. The pedestal table, stamped by Gaspard Schneider, is decorated with bronzes by P.-P. Thomire and arabesques painted by Jean-Jacques Lagrenée the Younger. It was created in 1786 to support a Sèvres porcelain plate. Above it is a gilded ebony and bronze writing case bearing the marks of the Queen's furniture store at Trianon.

A corridor to the left
of the fireplace leads back
to the grand stairway,
from where it is lit.
This corridor leads
to a dressing room
with chairs and a bathroom
converted in 1837 for
the Duchess of Orleans;
the bathtub dates
from this period.
Here you can see
a rare Japanese varnished
chest circa 1640, confiscated
from the Prince de Condé
at Chantilly in 1794.

The antechamber has a sérancolin marble fireplace which is less modern than that on the first floor. Even some window-frames removed in 1765 from the Parisian hotel of the Marquise de Pompadour, the present Élysée Palace which she bequeathed to the King, have been used again on this level. To the right of this window, the large upright clock, created by Robert Robin in 1787, was bought by Louis-Philippe in 1837. Above the chest of drawers by J.-F. Leleu hangs a marble medallion showing a profile of Marie-Antoinette, dated 1774 on the reverse and attributed to Augustin Pajou.

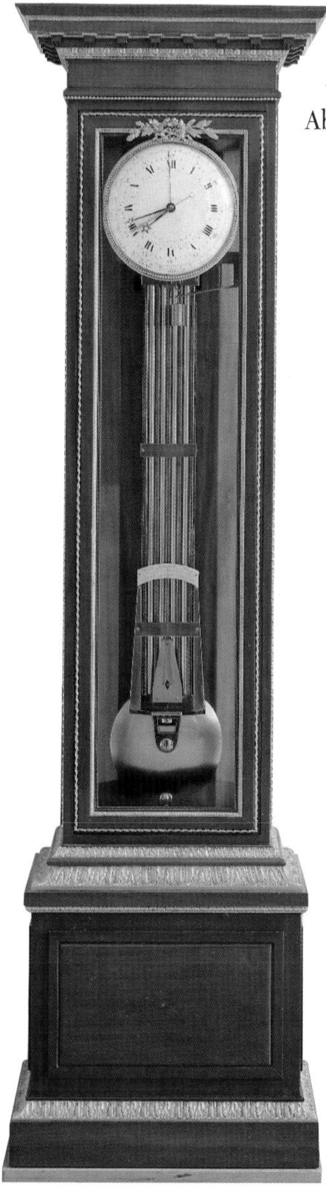

The gilded bed "à la polonaise" (in the Polish style) carved with lion muzzles replaces the bed "à la turque" (in the Turkish style), also gilded, created by the Foliots. The chairs by J.-B.-C. Sené formed part of the games room of Louis XVI at Compiègne, furnished in 1790.

The varnished chest of drawers supplied by G. Joubert in 1768, the whereabouts of which are currently unknown, has been replaced provisionally by a chest of drawers plated with polished metal, stamped by Pierre Macret and bearing the marks of the furniture store of the Dauphine Marie-Antoinette. It supports a Sèvres porcelain group created in 1781 by L.-S. Boizot to commemorate the birth of the dauphin (this is a 19th century copy; the original plaster cast is exhibited in Louis XVI's chamber at Versailles).

The King's bed chamber has just been restored to its state at the time of the Ancien Régime, except for the Italian griotte marble fireplace with gilt bronze reliefs, which was not added until 1836. The fireplace came from one of the small apartments of Marie-Antoinette at Versailles which were dismantled on the orders of Louis-Philippe. The three glass overmantels were restored in 1985 from designs found on the masonry. The crimson and white lampas "in the Chinese music style" is a reference to the style of the furniture delivered for Louis XV in 1768 and preserved by his successor. None of the original furniture has been found.

Located at the corner of the former Botanical and Flower Gardens, this is the only room to have been refurnished for Louis XVI in 1777. Most of the cabinets supplied by Riesener are preserved in foreign collections. The marquetry writing desk with flower medallion was supplied in 1784 by Riesener to the Queen's furniture store whose mark it bears along with the mark of the Chateau de Trianon; it was probably intended for Madame Élisabeth. The Belvedere, which can be seen from the window, was the subject of the painting by Claude-Louis Châtelet exhibited above the chest of drawers (see page 11). The artist painted it in 1781 on the occasion of its illumination during the summer by the Queen. The next room, reached through a door opened in the 19th century, is no longer part of the King's apartment.

The chair was created in 1780 by the Foliots after the designs of the architect Jacques Gondouin, who was also designer for the royal furniture store. It was part of the furniture delivered in 1781 for the drawing room of the Belvedere in the English Garden.

The six other attic apartments were intended by Louis XV for members of the nobility, including the captain of the guards. At the centre of the pavilion, the rooms without exterior windows were intended for the footman and the valet. As Madame de Pompadour died in 1764, nothing was planned for her or for a new mistress at the time when the furniture was commissioned in 1767-1768. It was therefore a nobleman's apartment which was occupied first of all by the Comtesse du Barry, for whom a more feminine suite of furniture was provided in 1770, along with the former folding chaise d'affaire of the late Marquise. In 1782, Marie-Antoinette had three nobleman's apartments joined together to form an apartment for her daughter, Madame Royale.
As for Madame Élisabeth, sister of Louis XVI, she seems to have mainly occupied the apartment of the King.

The curators of the museum are now endeavouring to collect in these apartments, in the course of restoration work, various items of furniture supplied for the chateau in the 19th century for the benefit of the Empress Marie-Louise and then the Duke and Duchess of Orleans.

Upon leaving the chateau and immediately to their left, visitors are met by a gate leading to the gardens. They can begin their walk with the English Garden and Marie-Antoinette's Hamlet but if they start with the French Garden of Louis XV they will get a more accurate sense of the historical and artistic chronology, and will gain a better understanding of the evolution of the art of gardening, as perfectly illustrated by the Petit Trianon. To take the latter option, visitors should walk around the little chateau, lingering briefly to admire one of the oldest trees on the estate, the Japanese Sophora. The main terrace of the chateau overlooks the French Garden created by Louis XV in 1749 as a new menagerie and extended at the time of the building of the Petit Trianon. The garden unfolds into a long lawn with floral borders, interrupted by two circular ponds and, above all, by a pavilion in the shape of a Saint Andrew's cross, framed on both sides by alleys of lime trees and a succession of green rooms laid out in the arbours. The alley to the left, which also serves the steps, allows access to the tribune of the chapel which borders the outbuildings constructed in 1770 and was extended in 1781 for Marie-Antoinette, to the detriment of the initial plan which originally included a compost garden, a fig orchard, a henhouse and an aviary.

The Marquis d'Argenson, former minister of foreign affairs to Louis XV, wrote in December 1749, "A new menagerie is being built at Trianon, but it seems to be more in the way of a practical menagerie than merely an object of curiosity, with a large dairy, many hens and a number of beautiful cows from Holland."

The prospect is interrupted at its centre by the "New Menagerie Pavilion", better known as the French Garden Pavilion or simply the French Pavilion. It was erected between 1749 and 1750 by A.-J. Gabriel. Jules Antoine Rousseau, sculptor of the King's buildings, created the groups of children and vases of flowers which used to surmount the balustrade, concealing the roof (those visible today are modern replacements). Designed as an octagonal drawing room flanked by four annexes (an antechamber, a conversation room, a dressing room with chairs, and a réchauffoir), the pavilion is located, like a belvedere, at the intersection of the main paths.

The most striking feature of the interior is the cornice supported by eight Corinthian columns and decorated with farmyard birds, recalling the neighbouring menagerie (pigeons, cockerels, hens, ducks and swans). It is perhaps better to forget the gilding added in the 19th century and out of keeping with the spirit of the place - Louis XV preferred assorted rustic colours on furniture upholstered with material and painted pekin on yellow, blue and green woodwork. Porcelain flowers also decorated the lights here.
In the summer, one could marvel at leisure at the beautiful floor comprising various different marbles: blue-veined, red Languedoc, turquin blue, Campan green, and Italian griotte. In the winter, it was covered with a Savonnerie carpet designed specially after a circular plan by J.-B. Chevillion. Marie-Antoinette often used the French Pavilion with an adjoining collapsible marquee for her parties and balls.

Built between 1778 and 1780 to replace one of Louis XV's first hothouses, and concealed by the hill in the F Garden and the li trees of the Frenc Garden, the exter of this theatre was given exceptionall exotic decoration by its architect Richard Mique, the successor to Gabriel. He there paid all the more attention to the m visible entrance - two Ionic columns framing a doub door and supporting the pediment sculpted by Joseph Deschamps of Apollo as a child, between the emblems of tragedy and comedy. Mique made for this in the interior of the theatre (which can be s on conference visits). His sumptuous decoration is designed entirely in pasteboard in a harmonious ble of blue and gold, on a false white-veined marble background. The ceiling, commissioned from J.-J. Lagrenée the Younger in 1779, portrays Apollo, the Graces, Thalia, Melpomene and the Renommée (figure of a winged woman blowing a trumpet). Marie-Antoinette, who loved these spectacles, had no hesitation in treading the boards of this new stage straight away, together with volunteers chosen from the royal family and various members of her "clique".

The groups of children on the arches and all the front-of-stage decoration crowned with two muses flourishing the monogram of the Queen are also by Joseph Deschamps. The great lateral candelabra adorned with cornucopia-bearing women, are exceptional in that they were not sold during the Revolution.

To protect visitors from inclement weather, a collapsible corridor linked the theatre to the small chateau and followed the alley between the arbours. Visitors come upon a small "roundabout" replanted in 1992 to commemorate the ring game built on this spot in 1776. The merry-go-round was driven by two men in a ditch underneath the ride. A. Bocciardi was responsible for carving the three Chinese figures supporting the pole, the two dragons of the weather-vane and the eight seats of the merry-go-round, four shaped like dragons for the men, and four shaped like peacocks for the ladies. The mechanism was built by the engineer Perrier and the ironsmith Roche, who were happy to plagiarise the Duc de Chartres' game at Monceau, created by Pierre Deumier. In 1781, Marie-Antoinette had a semi-circular gallery built in trellis work decorated in the Chinese style, sheltering in the centre an oval room and, at each end, an octagonal room, all furnished with benches with interlacing. The following year, the ring game was linked with the chateau, as can still be seen today by the blocked-up door. It was sold in its entirety for a third of its value in 1794. In 1810, Napoleon ordered a new ring game for the Empress Marie Louise - this game disappeared around the middle of the century.

As soon as she became mistress of the estate, Marie-Antoinette expressed the wish to have a garden in the English, or "Anglo-Chinese" style, as it was then known. This involved applying the ideas of a return to nature, championed notably by Jean-Jacques Rousseau. Antoine, son of Claude Richard, who was more gardener than landscaper and technician than artist, undertook the first project which, while sacrificing, under orders, the botanical garden, remained too classical around the chateau in its recreation of French-style parterres, and appeared too confused in the English part. Disappointed, the Queen turned to a distinguished amateur, the Comte de Caraman, who designed a new project, the broad outlines of which were immediately adopted. A. Richard, R. Mique and soon the painter Hubert Robert, consulted on the subject of the viewpoints, all collaborated in its creation. This collection of talent created a new masterpiece, with which one must also associate explorers who, as in the time of Louis XV, continued to bring back trees and rare flowers from faraway countries. The English agronomist, Arthur Young, a materials specialist, convinced himself that this garden charmed the uninitiated as much as the initiated.

Visitors arriving from the French Garden come face to face with the northern façade of the chateau on the site of the former botanical garden, opposite the river. Visitors have a choice of two routes leading to the Temple of Love situated directly in line with the chateau. From the avenue on the right, visitors can see the Belvedere pavilion and the structure of the theatre, located to the side of the château.
Visitors can therefore immediately take in the three main monuments which Mique chose to decorate the English Garden.

The river leads to the Temple of Love, located on an island. This elegant domed rotunda rests on twelve Corinthian columns sculpted, like the frieze, by J. Deschamps and finished in 1778. It once housed the original, then the copy by Louis-Philippe Mouchy of the famous group by Edme Bouchardon, "L'Amour taillant son arc dans la massue d'Hercule" (Cupid cutting his bow from the club of Hercules), now at the Louvre. It is from this statue that the temple derives its name. The Temple of Love was one of the privileged locations for the nocturnal parties held on several occasions by Marie-Antoinette - for her brother Joseph II in 1781, to celebrate the peace with England in 1782, in honour of the King of Sweden in 1784. Its graceful silhouette stood out harmoniously against the flames of the fires maintained in the adjacent ditch, reinforced by the light of thousands of torches. Chinese lanterns and terrines concealed in the surrounding clumps of flowers would then illuminate the flowers as if it were broad daylight.

To reach the Hamlet, an ensemble of cottages built from 1783 on in the style of the Normandy countryside around a pond, visitors can take a long alley on the left, which crosses the river over a stone bridge and ends at the Great Lake, which is itself also artificial. Amongst the beautiful trees, visitors will notice on their left, a plane tree with ramified branches and trunk. The first cottage to appear is the mill, restored in 1994. Like most of the cottages in the Hamlet, the mill, with its thatched roof, is located in a small vegetable and flower garden enclosed by a trellis fence. A wooden bridge spanning the river allows visitors to view it face on and admire the paddle wheel.

Set back from the mill is the Boudoir, concealing behind a seemingly rustic appearance a dressing room and an elegant room carefully panelled in Dutch oak painted in a mahogany colour by Louis-Joseph Dutems, who also silvered the edges of the tapestries and the mirror frame. This frame was carved by J. Deschamps, just like the white marble sculpted fireplace decorated with a floweret, with entwined foliage, rosettes, piasters and trails of ivy.

At the time of Marie-Antoinette, hamlets were considered an absolute must for any fashionable garden, and as exotic for their indulged owners as faraway fantasies. They offered a change of scenery too mild to cause any anxiety, because, as soon as one crossed the threshold of the cottages, one rediscovered the luxury to which one was accustomed. In this regard, Marie-Antoinette followed the example of her entourage and her family, like the Prince de Condé at Chantilly. But she extended the game much further by associating these mock cottages with a real farm, with herself as its overlord. The cottages in the Hamlet awaiting restoration are not currently open to visitors.

The Queen's Cottage occupies a privileged position on the banks of the Great Lake. It is designed in two parts linked by a wooden gallery, and seems almost imposing in the context of the Hamlet.
The right-hand side accommodates the Queen's Cottage proper which, in contrast to the other buildings, has a tiled roof. The ground floor held a vast dining room, and the first floor had a nobleman's antechamber, the drawing room and a backgammon room. Once again, the panelling, cornices and white marble fireplaces were particularly well preserved.
The private furniture store of the Queen was intended for G. Jacob and J.-H. Riesener to supply beautiful furniture.
The left-hand side of the cottage accommodated, on the ground floor, the billiard room and, on the first floor, a series of small rooms, including a Chinese room.
All the balconies were decorated with flowers growing in Saint-Clément Lorraine earthenware tubs and pots with the monogram of the Queen.
Through the arcades of the ground-floor gallery, a third cottage can be seen, known as the Réchauffoir.
With its rather complex layout, this cottage served to accommodate the services of the adjacent dining room, including a linen store, a silver store and even a room for the footmen, all behind a rustic façade.

Crossing the river once again over a little stone bridge of especially elegant design, visitors arrive at the pigeon loft, which served for a time as a henhouse, then as an aviary. Behind it, in a large enclosure, is the guardhouse still inhabited by a gardener of the estate.
On the other side of the alley are two enclosures which surrounded the Grange until 1810, and served as ballroom and processing dairy - a low wall on the ground testifies to the existence of these former buildings.

"In the midst of this little Hamlet, a high tower, known as the Marlborough Tower, dominated its surroundings. Its exterior staircases, covered in wallflowers and geraniums, had an elevated parterre. One of the cottages contained the dairy, and the cream, stored in superposed porcelain vases on white marble tables, was chilled by a stream running through the room. Close by was the real farm where the Queen kept a magnificent herd of Swiss cows that grazed on the surrounding meadows."
Félix, Comte de France d'Hézecques, memoirs of a page at the court of Louis XVI.

On a headland advancing into the lake, complete with a landing stage, stands the Marlborough Tower, named after the English general, hero of a famous song. The tower commands the best view of the Queen's Cottage. It accommodates a fishery at its foot and adjoins the processing dairy (used for tasting) which, as such, benefited from sophisticated genuine or fake marble décor, fashioned by the marble mason Louis-François Lepince and painted by L.-J. Dutems, who also created the false ceiling and the caissons of the vault. In 1786, the porcelain workshop supported by the Queen in the rue Thiroux in Paris supplied terrines, cheese makers, butter dishes, pitchers, six plates and two butter churns. During the Revolution, the Dairy was torn apart like the other cottages in the Hamlet, but it was elegantly restored by the marble mason Pierre-Claude Boichard between 1811 and 1818. During this period, the white marble busts placed on stone plinths, which concealed the pipes supplying water to the building, were installed on each of the four sides.

Leaving the lake and turning inland, visitors walk along an avenue leading to the Farm. The farm was built after the other cottages, in 1784, and accommodated a genuine farmer and his wife from Touraine, together with their two children. Their task was essentially to provide the Queen with eggs, butter, cream and cheeses. Cows and goats bought for this purpose lived alongside various farmyard animals, including a pig. Having fallen into disrepair, the farm had to be rebuilt in 1958. It is currently given over to the Fondation Assistance aux Animaux (animal aid foundation), which in 1993, financed the meticulous restoration of the buildings and their interior and exterior fittings to accommodate a small collection of livestock. Children aged between five and twelve are welcome here during the week for educational visits.

Having walked around the farm, visitors cros
a vast area planted with magnificent trees, mainly comprised of conifers, which, in the 19th century, lent this part of the garden the nickname "Little Switzerland", accentuated by the fact that it ended at the artificial hill created for Marie-Antoinett
Several paths allow visitors to cross or walk along this artificial hill, but the loveliest vantage points are at its foot, on the banks of the river leading to the little lake in the direction of the Belvedere. Before reaching it along a winding path passing along Snail Hill, accessible via spiralling paths, visitors discover a small enclosed valle
leading to the Grotto, considerably cut back in the 19th century and closed off by a grille. It was here that on the afternoon of the 5th of October, 1789, the Queen received reports warning her that the people of Paris were marching on Versailles.

The Belvedere, together with the rock with a waterfall spouting from it, was erected by Mique on the hill in 1778, and its decoration was completed in 1781. J. Deschamps created the exterior decor, the four bas reliefs representing each of the seasons and those of the pediments, illustrating their attributes. The sphinxes on the steps, also by the same sculptor, were remade in 1894 by Carrez.

Inside, the stucco-work by Louis Mansiaux, known as Chevalier, was painted with arabesques by Sébastien-François Leriche, and, on the dome, J.-J. Lagrenée the Younger painted cupids in clouds. The floor was sump tuously paved. Its eight windows and French windows provided Marie-Antoinette with a panoramic view over her entire estate. Today, successive changes to the plantations and their growth have greatly diminished this effect. In July 1780, Louis XVI offered the Queen a suite of furniture specially designed by the Foliots after models by the architect Jacques Gondouin, designer for the royal furniture store, for this drawing room. Of this furniture delivered one year later when the Queen was pregnant with the Dauphin, the Versailles museum possesses one chair, exhibited in the Petit Trianon.

From the Belvedere, visitors can make their way directly to the Petit Trianon and the exit. They can also go back down on the opposite side to the Charpentier garden (from the name of the gardener who replanted it in 1850) an especially well tended area between Marie-Antoinette's orangery and the ivy-clad Richard House. Before the devastating storm in December 1999, some of the finest trees in the estate could be seen here; in the springtime, splendid rhododendrons and magnolias bloom here for a short time.

The grille to the right of the Richard House lets you to rejoin the alley passing under the bridge in the French Garden which leads to the esplanade of the Grand Trianon. Visitors taking this route will encounter many reminders of the age of Louis XV: the large Trèfle fishpond, then to the left and passing their enclosure, the thatched roofs of the two ice-houses (restored in 1982 and 1983). The last building is the French guardroom (as opposed to the Swiss guardroom), aligned with the new menagerie built by Gabriel. It shows an interesting range of windows from the 17th to 19th centuries. At the end, Louis XV authorised the construction of a small, charming residence intended for the Comte de Noailles, governor of Versailles.

Crédits photographiques :
RMN; Art Lys/Burnier/de Kerland/Février/Girard/Néri

Achevé d'imprimer le 28 juillet 2003
Imprimé en France
Dépôt légal : Août 2003